REMEMBER WHEN?

Remember When?

Joe Ralko celebrates his 20th anniversary writing nostalgia columns for The Senior Paper.

JOE RALKO

The Penny University Essays by Pete's Press

Contents

Dedication

This book is dedicated to the subscribers of
The Senior Paper
who have filled my heart with hope and joy for more
than two decades.

Praise from Subscribers
of The Senior Paper

I always find something informative in Joe's column.
> – *Gerald Richards, Brandon, Manitoba*

I have your column about open heart surgery before me. Thank you Joe for sharing that experience as well as your experience with the cancer. That's an enormous service you've done: SHARING
> – *Elaine Lawrence, Kelowna, B.C.*

I enjoy reading Joe's columns in *The Senior Paper* because the subjects are informative or funny. I like to read about the history of our country.
> -- *Lynnise Camire, Kenora, Ontario*

I too count every day in October with no snow as a blessing. I had to smile to myself when you wrote that you let the other drivers adjust to winter driving before you go out. . . My late mom, Nellie Trelenberg of the Bognor School District south of Kandahar, Sask., had a saying 'it has to snow three times before it stays.'
> – *Diane Robinson, Wadena, Saskatchewan*

I have known Joe for close to 70 years. Keep on writing Joe. You have found your niche in life!
>   *– Rick Zabloski, Cornwall, Ontario*

I'm 90 years old, have been receiving *The Senior Paper* for many years and look forward to reading it front to back every month. Many of these stories. . .keep my memories alive of how I grew up. Keep them coming, Joe! By the way I'm taking off my 75th harvest this year.
>   *-- Herman Kirstein, Raymore, Saskatchewan*

I have been receiving *The Senior Paper* for about five years and I really enjoy reading the stories that people write. I share them with my wife, and we have many laughs. I do especially enjoy your columns. I somehow identify with you about "using new technology."
>   *- Victor Koop, Stony Plain, Alberta*

INTRODUCTION

All of us enjoy a trip down memory lane occasionally to a very special place and time in our past.

Regardless of where you grew up in Canada, trips to "The Good Old Days" always bring a smile to our face when you think about a fond memory.

Since 1977, *The Senior Paper* has published stories by seniors about seniors.

The Senior Paper has evolved into a passionate community of like-minded people from coast to coast who love sharing their precious memories.

The paper is an echo chamber of nostalgia.

"We publish positive stories and heartfelt memories. Each issue is filled with a rich and vibrant history," says publisher Dennis Stacey.

"Real life stories are presented unvarnished by the people who experienced them and are wrapped around treasured photographic memories of the past and present day."

The purpose of Remember When? is to celebrate my 20th anniversary of being a part of *The Senior Paper* community.

Although written initially for the enjoyment of subscribers to *The Senior Paper,* the 25 columns selected for Remember When have themes that also appeal to a younger demographic (and the columns are also among my favourites!)

The columns in the book do not appear in the same chronological order in which they were published in *The Senior Paper.*

Over two decades, even while I faced some very serious health challenges -- I battled cancer twice; had open heart surgery; and had to teach myself how to walk again as a result of Vertigo – I never missed a deadline to submit more than 200 columns.

Proceeds from this book will be donated to the Canadian Cancer Society.

I hope many of these columns will help you Remember When?

Enjoy!

Joe Ralko
September 1, 2024

PART ONE

Chapter 1

Remember Singing 'CA-NA-DA . . .We Are 20million'?

Mention the name Bobby Gimby today and someone who was in school in 1967 will likely start singing the first lines of *"CA-NA-DA."*

If there are two or more about the same age in your group when his name pops up during a conversation, the younger people in the group will give you their "deer in the headlights stare" as you simultaneously begin to sing:

CA-NA-DA,

One little two little three Canadians,

We love thee!

Now we are 20 million!

CA-NA-DA,

Four little five little six little provinces,

Proud and free!

Now we are ten and the territories sea to sea!

Back in 1967, trumpeter Bobby Gimby had the entire country humming and thousands of kids marching down Main Street with his Centennial Song.

It was a simple marching song. Nothing too serious. Just something catchy that children, like me and you, could sing or shout in celebration of Canada's centennial.

As a Grade 7 student at Mount Carmel elementary school, I too was caught up in the hype of celebrating our country's 100th birthday.

However, what stuck in my mind most about Gimby' s song was the fact our population had hit 20 million!

Fast forward to about a year ago when Canada's population hit forty million.

There was no great celebration, no outpouring of celebrations from coast to coast, to share the fact our population had doubled in a little more than fifty years.

Canada's population is on the grow as a direct result of a federal government policy to open our border to more newcomers.

"Just over 1.2 million new immigrants settled permanently in Canada from 2016 to 2021, the highest number of recent immigrants recorded in a Canadian census," says the website for the federal immigration department.

"Almost one in four people (twenty-three per cent) counted during the 2021 census are or have been a landed immigrant or a permanent resident in Canada. That was the highest proportion since Confederation."

I also learned on the same website that Canada was to "welcome from 430,000 to 542,000 new permanent residents in 2024" and slightly more next year "from 442,000 to 550,000."

Those are big numbers but what does that mean?

For Canada to hit our low-end immigration target (430,000 more people), this would be like adding the populations of Kamloops and Prince George, B.C.; Medicine Hat, Alta.; Moose Jaw, Sask.; Brandon, Man.; Sault Ste. Marie, Ont.; and Fredericton, New Brunswick each year!

Or at the higher end of the target range (542,000 this year), imagine adding another Halifax plus Thunder Bay, Ont. and Nanaimo, B.C. in one year to our country's population.

I understand why Canada is opening our borders to more residents. However, I wish there were more detailed planning before the tsunami of people landed here.

The impact of this wave of newcomers is most visible in two areas: schools and health care.

Many school divisions and districts across the country have had to accelerate plans to expand schools and build new ones to accommodate the unprecedented newcomer student enrolment growth.

Where I live, Regina Public Schools created and built new classroom spaces for six thousand more students in the eight-year period ending 2020.

In health care, the challenge is to find someone who speaks the newcomers' language because often they have limited grasp of English or French.

It's important to put Canada's population into a global context.

Even though our population has doubled since the 1967 Centennial year, Canada's population is less than half a per cent (0.48 to be exact) of the world population.

I wonder what Bobby Gimby would say or sing about our population if he were alive today?

He might start by looking at how much his hometown of Cabri, Sask. has changed and is an example of Canada's growth.

The population of the town about a half hour's drive north of Swift Current has grown to almost five hundred from three hundred when we all learned to sing "CA-NA-DA!"

Chapter 2

Seniors Now Outnumber Children in Canada for First Time

Who are we?

Throughout this year, Statistics Canada has been releasing batches of information gleaned from last year's census and the data paints an interesting answer.

Notwithstanding that the mandatory long-form census was reinstated, Canadians responded at a remarkable rate – 98.4 per cent which is said to be the best recorded since the 1666 census of New France.

That was the first census conducted in Canada and the first in North America.

At that time, there were 3,215 people in New France.

Last year, there were 35,151,728 people who reported living in Canada on Census Day, May 10, 2016, and showed interesting patterns of population growth across the country.

To put that into perspective, Canada's population accounts for less than one half of one per cent of the world population.

It's just slightly more than the largest city in the world: Tokyo-Yokohama (33.2 million residents).

The population count in 2016 was ten times greater than in 1871, when the first census after Confederation recorded 3.5 million people in Canada.

By 1967, when we were celebrating one hundred years since Confederation that number had grown to twenty million, Statistics Canada reminds us.

Over the years, Canadians have been trekking west.

In 1871, most Canadians lived in the four founding provinces of Ontario, Quebec, New Brunswick, and Nova Scotia, while Western Canada was sparsely populated.

By 2016, almost one-third of the population lived in Manitoba, Saskatchewan, Alberta, and British Columbia. Not surprisingly, the bulk of the country's population is in Ontario and Quebec (three in five Canadians live there).

About two-thirds of Canada's population growth over the previous five years was the result of migratory increase. Natural increase (the difference between the number of births and deaths) accounted for the remaining one-third.

That tells me the future of our country requires more newcomers because of low fertility and an aging population.

Population density remains unchanged.

Two-thirds of Canadians still live close to the southern border. In 2016, two out of three people (66%) lived within one hundred kilometres of the southern Canada–United States border.

Canada has a small population living in a large land area (close to nine million square kilometres), resulting in a low population density compared with other countries.

For example, Canada had just 3.9 people per square kilometre in 2016, compared with 35.3 people per square kilometre in the United States.

Mumbai (which was called Bombay when I went to elementary school) with a population of 14.35 million people has a density of 29,650 people per square kilometre.

The Canadian population continues to be highly concentrated geographically. Population growth tended to be higher in the west and lower in the east.

The four western provinces were the only provinces to record population growth rates higher than the national average, Statistics Canada reported.

For me, the big news from the 2016 census was there now 5.9 million Canadian seniors, compared to 5.8 million Canadians aged fourteen or younger. That's the first-time seniors have outnumbered children in this country.

As a result, Statistics Canada predicted that by 2031, about 23 per cent of Canadians could be seniors, like Japan, the world's oldest country. By 2061, there could be twelve million seniors to just eight million children in Canada.

However, Alberta, Saskatchewan, and Manitoba, as well as the three northern territories, have more children than seniors.

The three Prairie Provinces also have more millennials (individuals 15 to 34) than baby boomers (51 to 70).

At almost 20 per cent, Atlantic Canada has the highest proportion of seniors in the country, while Alberta, at just over 12 per cent, has the lowest. That disparity between

Canada's oldest and youngest regions is the widest in the country's history.

Who are we?

We are Canadians!

Chapter 3

How Old Would You Be If You Didn't Know How Old You Are?

Because I turn sixty-five later this month, I've been thinking about "milestones" in my life for the past few weeks.

I'm uncertain when milestones switched from an age-based system (such as I can't wait until I'm sixteen, then I can get my driver's license) to personal achievements.

In my youth, forty was old and sixty-five was, well, real old.

I'm certain I won't feel any different when I reach that milestone.

It begs the question, first posed, I believe by Leroy "Satchel" Paige, an American baseball pitcher:

How old would you be if you didn't know how old you are?

Paige, at the age of forty-two, was the oldest major league rookie while playing for the Cleveland Indians. He became the first player who played in the Negro leagues to pitch in the World Series (1948).

Before some of you call the politically correct police, please stop. Back then, it was called Negro League Baseball, because Major League Baseball wasn't integrated yet.

I digress. Sorry.

Milestones always have been linked in my mind's eye to specific ages, not events.

To be honest, turning forty was more traumatic for me than turning sixty. I did feel I was "getting old and almost over the hill."

Was it because I was closer to sixty than sixteen?

Based on numerous articles I found on-line, I concluded milestones today are events in your life and not tied specifically to age.

Here are some examples that we can all relate to: your first day of school, your first kiss, falling in love and then the first time someone broke your heart, moving out of your parents' home, buying a car without having someone "co-sign" the loan or lend you money, getting married, buying a house, having a baby (or a grandchild) and reaching an age where you know how to admit when you're wrong.

Last year, I achieved a secret, personal milestone.

While training for what I decided would be my final season officiating high school basketball (I dubbed my farewell tour Geezerhood 2019 by the way), I set a goal of dropping back down to the same weight I was when I graduated from high school.

I was quite proud when I hit my target but made the mistake while running on a treadmill in the gym one day of telling a personal trainer who was walking past me.

"Hey Karlee, I've hit my goal -- getting back to the same weight I was when I graduated from high school," I huffed and puffed, trying not to do a face plant while talking to her and running on the treadmill.

She smiled, approached me, and asked: "When was that?"

Without thinking, I blurted the answer: "1973."

"Good for you, Joe," she replied. "By the way, my mom was born in 1974!"

At that moment, not only did I feel foolish for putting my foot in my mouth so to speak but I felt old – very, very old!

Back to Satchel Paige's rhetorical question: How old would you be if you didn't know how old you are?

For years, I couldn't figure out why my answer to that question was twenty-three.

Then it dawned on me (again, when I was lost in my own thoughts pounding away on the treadmill), that was my age when I moved to Saskatchewan! Time stood still after that.

Paige is also credited with several other age-related words of wisdom. Here are my favourites:

Age is a case of mind over matter. If you don't mind, it doesn't matter.

Don't look back. Something might be gaining on you.

Work like you don't need the money. Love like you've never been hurt. Dance like nobody's watching.

I will try to – especially after I turn sixty-five later this month!

Chapter 4

Millennials More Likely to be Scammed than Seniors

This morning, I had a cup of coffee with Karen Smith and Kristin Bend at the Better Business Bureau (BBB) office here in Regina.

My purpose was to learn about the Top 10 Scams so I could weave it into a warning column and a sort of "Christmas gift" from me to you.

I had thought I was going to be told criminals are the most successful scamming or conning (pick your verb) seniors and women.

However, the facts didn't support my theory.

I found some real surprises within the data gathered by the BBB: men were more vulnerable than women in seven of the top ten scam categories; and people eighteen to twenty-four (not sixty-five plus) were the most likely to lose money to a scam.

Younger consumers have a lower median loss than people in their top earning years, partly because the types of scams aimed at older consumers tend to have higher median losses.

While seniors also tend to lose more money than Millennials when they are scammed, they fall for scams far less often.

And the biggest takeaway -- *no one is immune from the risk posed by scams.*

Before I continue, let me tell you a bit about the source of my information.

The Better Business Bureau was founded in 1912 and is a nonprofit organization focused on advancing marketplace trust. It consists of one hundred and twelve independently incorporated BBB organizations in Canada, the United States and Mexico.

The nefarious Top 10 list of scams is an amalgamation of information gathered from the BBB's Scam Tracker website, the Canadian Anti-Fraud Centre and concerns brought forward by sponsors (like the RCMP and community partners).

The truth is, it's not good news and the numbers don't lie.

Canadians lost more money in 2016 (ninety one million dollars) than the previous two years – 2015 (sixty-one million dollars) and 2014 (seventy million dollars).

Yet, there was some good news.

The No. 1 scam from the previous year has been in decline.

That's because a telephone call centre in India was raided and the dreaded Canada Revenue Agency Tax Scam dropped off drastically (falling to number nine).

While the number of people taken by that scam remains down, it has not gone away entirely.

"There appears to be more reporting going on which would explain some of the increase in the money lost," said Smith, the Chief Executive Officer of the BBB of Saskatchewan.

"But at the end of the day, it still only represents at most five per cent of what was actually taken from Canadians."

Smith believes there is a lot more reporting to do.

"Don't be ashamed, let someone know if you've been scammed. Those that report are warning others and are heroes in my eyes."

The total number of BBB scam tracker reports (from Americans and Canadians) in 2016 was thirty-two thousand seven hundred and eighty-one with a median loss of two hundred and seventy four dollars.

For Millennials (eighteen to twenty-four year olds) the No. 1 scam was fake cheque/money orders while the fake family or friend emergency story was the No. 1 scam against people sixty-five years and older.

The riskiest scam types by gender: male – investment; female – online purchases.

Scams delivered by phone were the most frequently reported.

However, the combined total of the various forms of online scam delivery (such as e-mail, websites, social media platforms like Facebook and Twitter, online classifieds, Internet messaging) accounts for more than half of all reports of monetary loss.

The Top 10 scams of 2016 were: employment, romance, identity fraud, advance fee loans, online purchase, wire fraud, binary options scams, fake lottery winnings, Canada Revenue Agency taxes owed and fake online endorsements.

The numbers are being crunched as you read this for 2017, but that report won't be available until sometime during the first quarter of next year.

In the meantime, from our family to yours, have a Merry Christmas and a safe Holiday Season!

Chapter 5

Technology Can be Difficult to Master

Technology is great when it works.

When it doesn't, I automatically assume it's my fault!

I'm not afraid of technology.

It's just that, to badly paraphrase comedian Steve Martin "I'm not a handy kind of guy."

(Of course, loyal viewers of *The Saturday Night Live* television series recognize my paraphrase of Martin's hilarious skit in the 1970s: "I'm just a wild and crazy guy!")

Not only am I not handy "figuring things out" (looking at something electronic or mechanical and immediately identifying what's wrong) I am very bad at following written instructions.

I shutter when my wife returns from a shopping trip to announce: "Guess what we bought today?"

"Oh, no!" is what I think, but "That's great, let's try it out tonight" is what comes out of my mouth.

Happy wife, happy life.

Just reading instructions stresses me out because I'm a visual learner.

Show me how to do things – four, five or six times – and I'll inhale enough confidence and knowledge to give it a try, when no one is looking over my shoulder.

Not only do "new" things coming into our home stress me out but so does a "new and improved" item such as redesigned remote control for our cable television service (why do they always move so many of the buttons as well as rename the functions such as on/off to input?)

My arch enemy over decades have been "kitchen gadgets" that are advertised to make cooking easier and quicker.

Yeah, right.

Quicker only after I've spent hours figuring out how the darn thing works or to be honest that should read "how it is supposed to work."

Don't get me wrong.

I don't have technophobia. It's just that I'm not quick to embrace new technology.

"Technophobia is an extreme fear of technology," the Cleveland Clinic website tells us.

"People with technophobia may fear the power of artificial intelligence, robots, or computers. Technophobia is more than resistance to learning new technology."

The highly respected medical website goes on to say that people with the condition may obsess over technology or, they may go to great lengths to avoid incorporating technology into their lives.

"Anyone can feel afraid of or reluctant to use new technology," the website concludes which made me smile.

"When the fear interferes with your life, it may be technophobia."

I quickly lost my joy and smugness as I continued to read.

"Adults and especially seniors are more likely to develop technophobia."

The Cleveland Clinic says experts don't know exactly how many people have technophobia, but it's "more common in older adults."

Oh, no, I wondered, am I joining that group?

"Many people refuse to use technology as they age."

That comforted me because I don't refuse to use technology, I just want to be able to easily use it without stressing out and taxing my brain too much.

"There isn't a single cause of technophobia. Factors that can contribute to technophobia include general anxiety about the future and mass hysteria (remember the Y2K scare?) about technology unknowns."

At the moment my fear is how technology functions or more precisely how I'm supposed to know how to use things like an app (application) on my cell phone, the new remote control or the latest "kitchen gadget."

If I was much, much younger I'd be more concerned about Artificial Intelligence known as AI (machines that teach themselves human skills at lightning speed!)

Historians in years to come will look back (at the growth of AI and its infiltration into so many parts of our daily life) as the moment when civilization was transformed just like it was by fire, agriculture, and electricity.

Today's technology challenge for me is how to add the Uber Eats app onto my phone. Arggh!

Maybe I'll go "old school" instead and make myself a peanut butter and banana sandwich -- less stress plus I get to make my lunch with my own two hands!

PART TWO

Chapter 6

I See Leaves of Green in the Heart of Winter

Growing up my favourite colour was red.

However, after living most of my adult life in Saskatchewan, my favourite colour now is green especially as we approach the cold heart of winter that is called February.

During the inky darkness of a bitter but familiar Canadian winter's night I often retreat into my Happy Room in my mind's eye.

I see myself reading in what I call my "nest," built with blankets and cushions on our patio sectional.

Snuggled within my nest on our back deck in spring and summer evenings, I enjoy sunshine streaming from my left (west).

In front of me (north side of our city lot) is a chorus of green.

Because of the age and variety of the species of trees there are many shades of green as the ash, elm, maple, and poplars begin to bud, leaves reach maturity, and then prepare for winter with a communion of colour.

This is my Happy Place in real life.

My Happy Room is a place I created in my mind to visit during the dark days recovering from my two battles with cancer and open-heart surgery.

Linus in the *Peanuts* newspaper cartoon series many years ago had a security blanket.

I have a pair of security blankets: my Happy Room and my Happy Place.

To be honest, I need one or the other to cope with the extreme weather we have been having in recent years.

A tweet (a post on the social media platform called Twitter) from the Regina Weather Office (YQR weather) reminded us, the city experienced one hundred and six consecutive hours last February of minus forty-degree temperatures.

Oh, I thought, I'd better start thinking about my green Happy Place just in case the Polar Vortex wraps it's cold, ugly arms around us for yet another February.

At about the same time we were chilled to the bone in this country, California was experiencing yet another winter of battling massive forest fires.

A few months later, a Dome of Heat enclosed everyone from the Manitoba border to the coastline of B.C.

Lytton, a village in the Fraser River Canyon located about one hundred- and fifty-kilometres northeast of Vancouver, broke the record for the hottest temperature ever recorded in Canada for a third consecutive day on June 29, 2021, hitting a scorching 49.6 C.

This caught the eye of editors at *Forbes* magazine which published an on-line story under the headline: "Canada Has Never Been This Hot; We're Talking Death Valley Hot."

"Lytton recorded a blistering temperature of 121.1 (Fahrenheit) degrees, the hottest moment ever seen anywhere in Canada since record-keeping began," said the article on Forbes.com.

"Perhaps the most compelling illustration of just how hot this is for a little village in the great north, is the fact that nowhere else north of the thirty-seventh parallel — that's the border between Colorado and New Mexico or Utah and Arizona — has ever recorded a hotter temperature."

Yup, that's hot.

Then a few months later during the Christmas-New Year's period it was cold, so cold at least half of the Top 20 coldest places in the world on any given day during that time were in western Canada.

Here in Regina, December 28, 2021, was the coldest Dec. 28 in one hundred and thirty-seven years (minus 38.6 C, without windchill.)

One day Calgary was ranked ninth coldest in the world on the Weather Extremes Now website (www.wx-now.com)

To top things off it snowed before Christmas, and the snow stayed on the ground on Vancouver Island and the British Columbia lower mainland, including Vancouver. A rare experience for that part of the country.

Today, I can only dream of sunshine and heat as I prepare for the worst February can throw our way by dreaming of my Happy Place on our back deck and the lazy, hazy days of summer.

Chapter 7

Remember the Sights, Smells, and Sounds of Summer?

Yeahhh! It's summer.

However, depending on where you live you might be asking either:

"When is summer arriving?" or "Did I miss it again?"

Nevertheless, please join me in this stroll down memory lane recalling the sights, smells, sounds and tastes of summer.

Over the past several years, one of the few things that kept me motivated to get out of bed in the wintertime during those week-long blasts of Artic was recalling some of the fond memories of my favourite season.

Let's take a sentimental journey down memory lane (of my youth and perhaps yours).

Summer is the smell of a freshly cut lawn and the crispness of air after a rain.

Summer smells like honeysuckle and burgers, hotdogs, or steaks cooking on the grill.

It smells like Coppertone (to help you bronze) or Solar Caine if you forgot.

Summer sounds like bullfrogs and the clank of swing chains going almost — but never quite — so high that they wrap around the uprights.

Why is it, you can fall asleep to the sounds of crickets outside your screened window yet a solo from a mosquito in your house will make you toss and turn the whole night?

Summer looks like the pink polka-dots of Calamine after losing a battle with a mosquito or two.

Summer is the crack of a ball on a wooden bat; flip flops walking past you as you attempt to snooze at the beach or at a swimming pool; the crack and crash of a thunderstorm (of course supported by brilliant flashes of lightning).

Regardless of your age, there are many activities you can enjoy (and remember) during summer such as blowing bubbles, dandelions, and kisses, jumping in waves, and dangling your feet into the water (from a boat or dock or rocky shoreline).

Did you hop on your heels or bang the side of your head to release the water "trapped" in your ear.

I grew up in northwestern Ontario, where our backyard literally was a swamp and creek that "flowed" into a larger creek (not a river) and eventually Laurenson's Lake, about three kilometres away.

One summer's day when our neighborhood gang of kids was about ten or eleven years old, we decided to build a flat-bottomed boat from scrap lumber we could find.

We did it.

To operate, however, it took four people: one to paddle and three to bail.

We'd eventually make it down the creek to Sedesky Point.

We knew we were foolish, but we were smart enough not to venture past Sedesky Point and into the lake "just in case" our boat fell apart!

I'm sure you each have had similar adventures in your youth, right?

Summer tastes like watermelon and an ice-cold popsicle right out of the freezer.

Summer feels like mud between your toes or a bee sting after running barefoot across your lawn or garden or fallow field.

One of the craziest "games" we invented as kids one summer, was killing bees by clapping our hands together.

The secret of success in that game -- which we didn't teach those who arrived late for our neighborhood gang fun -- was to clap your hands parallel to the ground, not perpendicular (up and down) so you would stun or kill the bee without getting the stinger embedded in the palm of your hand!

Summer is enjoying a drink of cold water from the neighbor's garden hose and watering the flowers or vegetable garden (with your parents or grandparents) and then, of course, watching them grow like magic.

Because I loved going to the well and bringing back a pail to fill up our watering cans as a kid, it just didn't "feel the same" when I grew up to use sprinklers!

Summer is wiener roasts that became marshmallow torch parades. (Sound familiar?)

We all have many fond memories of summer.

Go make some more!

Chapter 8

October Can be Great but Winter is Coming!

Like many Canadians, I secretly dread this time of year. We love the sights, the sounds, the smells of autumn.

We love the communion of colours as leaves magically change from green to brown, red, or orange.

We love the crunching of the dried leaves as we stroll through a park or down a sidewalk or along a hiking trail.

We love the smell of a crisp autumn rain or garden soil turned over to prepare for planting next spring.

However, there's a lingering certainty in the back of our minds that can surface in an instant and fill us with dread.

Winter is coming.

Depending on where you live in Canada, winter may arrive sooner than later. Or it may have already blanketed your community, your farm, or your home.

We love experiencing those rare and precious autumn days when the temperature can sore to summertime levels because we know the No. 1 certainty in Canada: Winter is coming.

Benjamin Franklin, the American diplomat, entrepreneur, and inventor, carved a wide swath through the pages of history.

He was brilliant with a sharp tongue.

"There are two certain things in life: death and taxes," Franklin is famous for saying.

As a Canadian, I know there's a third certainty that we all face at this time of year:

Winter is coming.

Don't get me wrong.

I like winter – eventually.

However, at this time of year I want what my neighbor Murray, a retired firefighter, describes as "more bonus days of summer."

"Even if those days are cold, damp and rainy?" I asked him once when he was walking his youngest daughter's dog Geronimo (nicknamed Gero).

"Yes, even those days are better than blizzards, snow drifts and minus 30-degree weather," he replied, double timing to keep up to the tiny dog that had darted across the street into Munro Park.

Winter is coming.

Murray and I have different definitions of when bonus days begin.

Every day without snow after the Labour Day Weekend are bonus days of summer for Murray.

For me, my threshold is the following month -- Thanksgiving Weekend – and then I keep my fingers and toes crossed for a snowless Halloween.

I'm not a total grinch about winter. I still enjoy tobogganing with our grandchildren, our adult-age children, and my wife.

Making snow "families" to represent ours, our children and their children and their pets (dogs and horses) can be a fun-filled afternoon.

I love to curl up with cup of tea and read a book beside a crackling wood fire in our living room as the snow gently glides to the ground outside – but please, not in October.

I'm never one hundred per cent ready when winter arrives.

In fact, for the past several years I have hidden in our house for a few days after the first snowfall hits us and stays.

That's because I want the other drivers to get used to winter-like conditions so there's less likelihood of a collision with me. It might be warped logic on my part, but it is a plan that has been effective so far.

I'll do my errands such as grocery shopping or picking up my medications when there should be a minimum number of vehicles slip, sliding around on the streets.

That means leaving our home after the morning rush hour has ended but returning well before the noon hour burst of activity from businesses and schools.

Depending on where you live in North America, October can be a very be enjoyable and pleasant month. Or it can hit you like a snowball in the back of your head.

Admit it.

You too secretly dread this time of year, even if it's a tiny thought dancing in the back of your mind.

Whether you like or dislike winter, it is a certainty in Canada. So, get ready to embrace it.

Winter is coming!

Chapter 9

Worst Part About Winter – Fewer Hours of Daylight

As a kid, I loved December.

I couldn't wait for Christmas Day, sharing gifts, eating lots and lots of food, and then being away from school allowed us to spend more time playing: outside (tobogganing down Zabloski's hill or walking to Central Park for a hockey game on the outdoor rink) or inside (learning how to play the new board games we had received as presents).

However, as an adult, I've grown to hate December so much it has become my least favourite month.

The worst part about winter in Canada is not coping with a Polar Vortex or the blizzards or freezing rain (depending on where you live).

For me, it's the reduced hours of daylight.

On Christmas Day last year here in Regina, the sunrise was at 8:58 a.m. and the sunset came at 4:58 p.m. That's not a lot of daylight (only eight hours) and a lot of darkness (16 hours!) to go with the winter weather.

I am not relishing the thought of driving to work this month in the dark and then driving home at supper time, again in the dark!

I lie to myself and say I can handle the cold by either adding more layers of clothing or simply staying inside.

After enduring the limited hours of sunshine in December last year, most of Canada was hit by a Polar Vortex (who thinks of these names?).

It was the coldest February in 83 years in Saskatchewan. Other parts of the country apparently were not much better!

According to Environment and Climate Change Canada, the last time there was a stretch of similar February temperatures in Regina was in 1939.

What does that mean?

In a "normal year" the daily highs would have been in the minus single digits and lows in the minus teens. Many days we experienced temperatures 20 degrees below normal.

Each of those bone-chilling February days, for me, however, were more and more tolerable because "the days got longer" (technically a day is still 24 hours, but what the expression captures is the fact we began to receive more hours of sunshine).

Spring forward fall back was the phrase drilled into us by the nuns at Mount Carmel elementary school in Kenora, Ont. to remind us of what to do with our clocks beginning and ending Daylight Savings Time (DST).

The main purpose of Daylight-Saving Time (called "Summertime" in many places in the world) is to make better use of daylight.

The theory behind DST is to change clocks during the summer months to move an hour of daylight from the morning to the evening.

Saskatchewan is the only province in Canada that does not have DST. In fact, there are many towns and villages across this country that don't switch to Daylight Saving Time from Standard time as well.

By the way, I've lived in Saskatchewan so long that the only way I notice the rest of the world has switched to Daylight Savings Time is because my favourite television shows are broadcast an hour earlier!

From my elementary school geography class, I know that if you live near the equator, day and night are nearly the same length (12 hours). But everywhere else on earth, there is much more daylight in the summer than in the winter.

The closer you live to the North or South Pole, the longer the period of daylight in the summer.

We were caught off guard the first year we lived in Prince Albert, Sask. (which is about 300 kilometres north of where I sit today).

It was very difficult to get our sons who were in Kindergarten and Grade 1 to stop playing outside because the sun was still up when it was their bedtime!

Can someone please think of how to create Winter Savings Time, to give us more hours of daylight, especially in December which would help me cope with the next Polar Vortex to descend upon us!

Chapter 10

Christmas Shopping Has Changed Dramatically in Our Lifetime

It is difficult to explain the excitement and joy of receiving the full-colour glossy Eaton's Christmas catalogue in the mail to someone who does their shopping by tapping on the screen of a cell phone with a bowl of popcorn on their lap!

The catalogue shopping process was the same if you lived in Vernon, B.C., Portage la Prairie, Manitoba, or Halifax, N.S. What varied was where you picked up your packages.

We had an Eaton's store in my hometown (Kenora, Ont.) so when the mail order arrived, we received a telephone call inviting us to "come downtown, pay, and pick it up."

The Senior Paper has published many stories over the years from readers about shopping for Christmas presents with the Eaton's catalogue.

Many of us fondly recall spending hours and hours looking for Christmas presents to "ask for" or "to give."

The worst part was completing the order form, double and triple checking the "numbers" to ensure you were purchasing the exact item, colour, and size you wanted. Your order then was in the hands of the postal service. You waited and waited to be notified of its arrival.

It's a far cry from Christmas shopping options now available – online or in person if the store is still open during the pandemic.

Technology has made shopping today easier, quicker, and often a lot more frustrating. Yet, it has tilted the playing field, so to speak, in favour of companies selling products vs. consumers like me looking for items to buy.

Coding on a website identifies each unique visitor.

So, if you are shopping for a specific brand of winter boots or parka, it's not an accident that an advertisement for that product or store pops up the next time you visit a social media page such as Facebook or Twitter.

In addition, if you "log in" to a company's website (read on-line store) with your email address just looking for ideas of what to buy, you likely will receive emails (often with discount coupons) promoting that product you had been looking at or similar products in the clothing or hardware department (wherever you were on their website).

Payment is the last step of the online ordering process.

In the past, we paid when we received our mail-order package.

The tools and techniques to push products at consumers via the World Wide Web makes advertising when I was a teenager seem like the Dark Ages.

A right of passage for teenagers, notwithstanding where we grew up in Canada, was the group car rides on the weekend.

Somebody would get their parent's car. Then, four, six, or eight of us would stuff ourselves into the vehicle and drive around listening to the radio, looking for friends in other cars who were also cruising Main Street or the "downtown" area of our tiny town.

Now, imagine hearing a commercial on your favourite radio station, then changing channels and the same commercial is playing there, change again and the commercial is also there!

That's how sophisticated online marketing has become.

Move from website to website and the same advertisement pops up on your screen!

To continue my analogy, when our friends in the other vehicle were spinning their radio dial, they could be getting a commercial on each station but for something completely different than what we did!

Target marketing, retargeting, cookies, geofencing are terms that I hear used to describe social media advertising techniques.

I understand the basics but find it too creepy because products are being pushed hard at consumers (me) wherever I go online.

On the other hand, our oldest son loves shopping online and the tracer ads because sometimes he'll be searching for something, get sidetracked, forget about it and then a few days later that "nice reminder" comes up and he pick ups where he left off.

Call me old school.

I miss my Eaton's catalogue.

PART THREE

Chapter 11

So, Do You Know Your Canadian History?

To help you prepare to celebrate Canada's 150th anniversary, two years from now, let me challenge everyone with ten questions about our great country.

I'm hopeful that most of you will get one hundred percent on what I consider to be a basic general knowledge test about Canada.

If not, perhaps you'll have something new to share with your friends and family over coffee or the backyard fence. Or you can share your concern as a Letter to the Editor or an email directly to me.

Because of my giddy, coffee-fueled mood today, I warn you there will be several trick questions. So, beware!

Question 1:

When did Canada adopt our flag consisting of a red field with a white square at its centre, in the middle of which an eleven-pointed, red maple leaf is featured?

This flag made its first official appearance on Feb. 15, 1965. Prior to that date, the Canadian Red Ensign had been unofficially used since the 1890s.

Question 2:

When did *O Canada* become our official national anthem?

It was proclaimed Canada's national anthem on July 1, 1980, more than one hundred years after it was first sung on June 24, 1880.

Question 3:

Canada has two official languages – English and French – but how many provinces are officially bilingual?

New Brunswick is the only bilingual province in Canada.

Nova Scotia, by the way, has a few bilingual laws – some are written in English and French and at least one is in English and German!

Here's a trick question, he hinted.

Question 4:

Name the three provinces that united in 1867 to form a new country.

Believe it or not the answer is New Brunswick, Nova Scotia, and the province of Canada, which on formation of Canada, was divided into Ontario and Quebec.

Question 5:

Which provinces subsequently joined Canada?

Manitoba entered confederation on July 15, 1870. Almost a year later, British Columbia became part of Canada, and then Prince Edward Island entered confederation on July 1, 1873.

Alberta and Saskatchewan were created as Canadian provinces on the same day in 1905, while Newfoundland and Labrador didn't join our country until 1949.

Question 6:

How many territories do we now have and name them?

We now have three territories: The Northwest Territories, Nunavut, and Yukon. By the way, did you know that Nunavut is the largest, newest, and northernmost territory of Canada. It was separated officially from the Northwest Territories on April 1, 1999.

The creation of Nunavut resulted in the first major change to Canada's political map since the incorporation of the new province of Newfoundland and Labrador in 1949.

Question 7:

Is lacrosse or ice hockey Canada's "official" game?

Another trick question because the answer is both!

In 1994, Parliament passed Canada's National Sport Act which declared lacrosse to be Canada's national summer sport and hockey as the national winter sport.

Now, this, for me, is always the most embarrassing question.

Question 8:

When did we get our own constitution?

We were governed under the British North America Act of 1867 until the Canada Act of

1982 was passed.

Question 9:

The official animal of Saskatchewan is the white-tailed deer and it's the Plains bison for Manitoba, but does Canada have an official animal?

Yes, Parliament made the beaver an official emblem of Canada in 1975.

Question 10:

What does our official motto – a Mari usque ad Mare – mean and in what language is it?

In Latin, it means from sea to sea.

Ironically, Canada borders on three oceans – Arctic, Atlantic, and Pacific – not two seas.

Only in Canada, eh?

Chapter 12

Happy Sixteenth Birthday to Me!

Happy sixteenth birthday Joe from yourself 50 years in the future!

You are not going to believe how many things have changed between 1970 and today.

During the Christmas holidays, I shocked our children and many of our in-laws when I confessed, I had no desire to listen to a "podcast," adding that I am still so old-fashioned I prefer listening to our favourite local AM radio station.

This drew immediate laughter and guffaws from the group.

What 1970 Joe needs to know is that 50 years into the future there has been a dramatic change in technology which is most notable in the entertainment industry.

A telephone is no longer something mounted on the wall that comes in one colour, black. Television is not a big heavy box sitting in the living room.

The number of people who listen to their "hometown radio station" is fewer than ever because there are so many options (podcasts, etc.) 24 hours a day seven days a week targeting specific audiences. Want to listen to your favourite country singer (Garth Brooks)? Connect with his own radio station via satellite.

I don't understand the complete range of technology but let me just simply say you can listen to a station playing music or sports or talk radio in new cars or while walking down the street using a device no larger than the palm of your hand.

It's commonly called a cell or mobile phone, but it's really a small portable computer with the telephone only one of many applications (things it can do).

Radio has come a long way since you were in Kenora, Ont. listening to CJRL-AM, a radio station that literally signed on the air at 6 a.m. and stopped broadcasting at midnight.

That black telephone mounted on the living room wall was replaced by wireless devices that fit into the palm of your hand.

Called cell phones by many people, it's really a portable computer because the "telephone" is only one part of dozens of functions or apps (applications) available including camera and video (Whatsapp).

No more waiting until after 6 p.m. or Sunday to make a "long distance" phone call.

People whip out the cell phone, tap it and connect with their friend or family member (who has the same app on their device) and may be in the same community or halfway around the world in places like Australia, India, or Nepal!

Sounds like a scene from the science fiction TV series *Star Trek* or the cartoon show *The Jetsons,* doesn't it? It's not. It's reality and an everyday part of our lives now.

Air to fill up the tires of your bicycle, car or truck is no longer free. It usually costs $1, which now is a coin and not paper money!

There have been major changes in laws.

It's illegal to smoke in bars and restaurants, most public buildings, and sporting events, but you can now smoke cannabis (which you called dope, pot or weed) in public and at home.

In 1974, Canada converted to the metric system (water freezes at zero degrees Celsius rather than 32 degrees Fahrenheit.) As a result, I confess I still don't really understand the mileage my car makes because fuel is measured in litres (not gallons) and distance in kilometres (not miles.)

The average price of a gallon of gasoline in Canada as you turn 16 is 36 cents per gallon.

Last summer, I paid $1.33 per litre when I filled up during a vacation in B.C. That's over $5 per gallon!

The only thing that hasn't changed in 50 years is that regardless of where you live in Canada, we still have only two seasons – winter and construction!

Enjoy the day. Get ready for a fast-paced life and a future in which you live in four provinces, settle in Regina, raise six children and, so far, have three grandchildren!

Happy sixteenth birthday Joe!

Chapter 13

Inventions and Other Stuff You Ought to Know About Canada, eh?

We are all proud Canadians, especially on July 1st.

To help you brag at your backyard barbecue or your community's Canada Day celebration, here is some "stuff" I found interesting and thought you ought to know about Canada – from basic facts about our country to inventions.

Let's start with geography, my all-time favourite subject in elementary school.

We all agree that it can get very cold in the winter, regardless of what part of this nation you call home.

An on-line article in the venerable *Readers Digest* reported the temperature in Snag, Yukon, on Feb. 3, 1947, was minus sixty-three Celsius or minus 81.4 Fahrenheit.

This might be real; might be fake news; or might simply be an equipment error. If it is true, that's the same temperature as the surface of Mars!

Canada has ten per cent of the world's forests and five hundred and sixty three lakes larger than one hundred square kilometres. The Great Lakes alone contain about eighteen per cent of the world's fresh lake water.

Canada is bigger than the European Union, three times the size of India, five times the size of Mexico and thirty per cent larger than Australia.

Bordered on three sides by three different oceans: the Atlantic, Arctic and Pacific, Canada has the world's longest coastline.

Canada accounts for 202,080 (or fifty-six per cent) of the world's total 356,000 kilometres of oceanfront property. The only other country that comes close is Indonesia, which has 54,716 kilometres of coastline.

Some of the greatest Canadian inventions have been in food and agriculture: an early form of peanut butter was first patented by Marcellus Gilmore Edson (1884); canola, McIntosh red apples, instant mashed potatoes, Canada Dry ginger ale, poutine, the Nanaimo bar, and butter tarts.

Our contributions in the communications and entertainment industries include: the Imax movie system; the walkie-talkie, Standard time, the Blackberry, and a pager.

In transportation and mobility, Canadians invented the first wheelchair accessible bus and the electric wheelchair, overhead power connection for electric street cars, the snowmobile, the crash position indicator (frequently called "the black box" in movies and television dramas about airplane crashes), snowblower and electric car heater (of course).

Canadians contributed to the world of sports inventing: basketball, ice hockey, five-pin bowling, and the tabletop hockey game. The instant replay was invented for CBC television's Hockey Night in Canada (1955).

Around the house, Canadians have provided you with the electric oven (and Easy Off cleaner), the garbage bag, caulking gun, paint roller, Robertson screw (and screwdriver) and egg cartons.

Canada, in many parts of the world, is best known for our achievements in health care and medical research. Some of the most famous are: Three doctors from the Hospital for Sick Children in Toronto developed Pablum (1930) to prevent and treat rickets in children.

Since then, the popular baby food has gone on to improve the health of millions of children around the world and has led to ideas to help hundreds of millions more.

The first cancer patients to receive radiation (the cobalt bomb) treatment were in Canada (1951).

A process for extracting medical insulin to treat diabetes was invented by Canadians (Frederick Banting, Charles Best and James Collip) (1922).

A vaccine against Ebola, a rare and deadly virus, was developed by Canada's National Microbiology Laboratory (2014).

And, of course, Medicare was born in Saskatchewan on July 1, 1962.

It became the first government-controlled, universal, comprehensive single-payer medical insurance plan in North America.

Ten years later, all Canadians were covered by a medical insurance system born in the dust of the Prairies.

These are only a few of the interesting items I found to share with you.

Canada is a big country and Canadians, historically, are inventive people.

I'm proud to be a Canadian, eh, and so should you!

Chapter 14

How To Speak Canadian from Eh! To Zed

Because Canada has welcomed millions of newcomers over the past few decades, I thought I'd help with their transition in this month's column with some tips on how to speak "Canadian."

A is the first letter of the alphabet but "Eh!" is the Canadian expression that we receive the most flak from the rest of the world.

The last letter of the alphabet is pronounced Zed, not Zee.

The only exception is when we talk about one of my favourite American rock bands, *ZZ Top*. It would be just wrong and too weird to call them *Zed Zed Top*.

Eh is a magic word because by adding it to the end of the sentence you can engage in a conversation.

For example, "It's a nice day." Is a simple declarative sentence.

However, "It's a nice day, eh?" is a question that encourages the other person to respond – "Yes, it is. Much better than yesterday."

I agree with the blog called The Planet D which declared the Loonie "by far the silliest word for currency on the planet."

More than thirty years ago this one-dollar coin was minted to replace the dollar bill.

Dollar coin just didn't roll off the tongue.

Instead, someone (I don't know who and searches on Google proved fruitless), somewhere decided the dollar coin should be called a Loonie because it had a picture of the loon on it.

Okay, as a Canadian I get that.

What I don't get is why the same rule didn't apply for naming the two-dollar coin, which came out several years later, a Bearie because of the picture of a polar bear is on it.

Nope, instead, it's a Toonie because that rhymes with Loonie.

It took me years to get the spelling correct. I thought it was twonie because it was a two-dollar coin.

During a high school trip to London and Vienna for the Easter break, I got the craziest looks when I asked directions to the "washroom" on a train or in a restaurant.

You go in a "WC" I was told, which later I learned was an abbreviation for Water Closet.

Canadians have our own way of referring to food and beverages: double double; "I'm at Tim's;" 24 (pronounced two-four); 26-pounder; Mickey; and Molson muscle come to mind.

"I'm at Tim's having a double double" means you are drinking a coffee with double cream and double sugar at your favourite Tim Horton's. This assumes the other person knows which is your favourite Tim's location.

Slang I once used to describe the size of a bottle of alcohol, or a box of beer has become outdated because the merchandising has changed.

You now can buy beer in single cans/bottles, a six-pack, fifteen and eighteen, more than just a dozen and a twenty-four.

The metric system has killed the phrase 26-pounder, which when I was growing up, was the middle of three size of bottles of spirits such as rye, rum, or vodka.

Beyond the 26-ounce bottle, the other sizes were 12-ounce, affectionately called a Mickey which you could slip it into your coat pocket, or the big 40-pounder the slang for a 40-ounce bottle. Spirits now are measured in milliliters not ounces.

Friends who drink and eat a lot often proudly refer to their "beer bellies" as Molson Muscle.

These are some of the key phrases to help newcomers to Canada.

Keep it handy because the number of immigrants will continue to increase.

Immigration accounts for almost one hundred per cent of Canada's labour force growth, says a story on the Reuters news wire.

"Roughly seventy-five percent of Canada's population growth comes from immigration," it said.

"By 2036, immigrants will represent up to thirty per cent of Canada's population, compared with 20.7 per cent in 2011."

These newcomers will need to learn how to speak Canadian, eh.

Chapter 15

Toast Your favourite Canadian This Summer!

I'll let you in on a secret: on Canada Day I'm going to hoist a few brews this summer in honour of a pair of very interesting Canadians who passed away during the past year.

Frank Ogden and 'Stompin' Tom' Connors were as different as day and night, yet their lives reflect the nature of what makes Canada a great country. They were unique and passionate about their work and the people who call Canada home.

Ogden was a futurist and wrote twenty-two books about how technology would change our lives.

Known as Dr. Tomorrow, Ogden predicted in *The Last Book You'll Ever Read,* we would "curl up with our computer or other electronic device on our bed."

I had the privilege of giving him a tour of the Prince Albert pulp and paper complex in 1989 when he told me about his 'upcoming' book project. I laughed because I didn't think it was possible.

Technology today has validated Ogden's vision. He lived a full and varied life before passing away at the age of ninety-two.

In 1953, he broke the Canadian light-plane altitude record by flying a Mooney M-18 Wee Scotsman to an altitude of nineteen thousand four hundred feet. With a conventional internal combustion engine, he set this "impossible" record by flying up until he ran out of gas and then gliding back to the airport.

At the time, Ogden joked that he was able to break the record because "most pilots are sensible enough to want twenty to thirty 30 gallons of gas left in the tanks to get back."

When he wasn't roaming the planet, Ogden worked from home on his wired houseboat in Vancouver's Coal Harbour.

He was a pioneer in streaming live video Internet broadcasts. From his floating electronic cottage, Ogden conducted the first two international seminars via satellite and fibre optic technology, for Australia's Telstra Communications Network in Sydney and Melbourne.

Years before he started using the Internet to stream live video, Ogden predicted that the broadcast universe wouldn't be limited to five hundred traditional channels, but would instead be a universe frequented by anyone with a camera, computer, and limited money.

It was one of his many predictions that he lived to see become a reality.

Ogden was also a fellow of the Explorers' Club, an elite group of adventurers that included mountaineer Sir

Edmund Hillary and astronauts Neil Armstrong and Buzz Aldrin.

At the other end of the Canadian cultural spectrum was Stompin' Tom Connors who passed away at age seventy-seven.

I never met "Canada's Man in Black" in person, but I did see him perform several times at Toronto's famous Horseshoe Tavern during the peak of his career in the 1970s.

Connors was one of Canada's most prolific and well-known country and folk singer-songwriters. He is credited with writing more than three hundred songs and released four dozen albums with total sales of nearly four million copies.

His songs reflect the pulse of Canada.

Three of his best-known songs — *Sudbury Saturday Night, Bud the Spud,* and *The Hockey Song*— play at every home game of the Toronto Maple Leafs hockey team. *The Hockey Song* is played at games throughout the National Hockey League.

Connors' habit of stomping the heel of his left boot to keep rhythm earned him his nickname. There are several theories about the origin of the foot stomping, but it's likely he did this to keep a strong tempo for his guitar playing especially in the noisy bars where he frequently performed.

After numerous complaints about damaged stage floors, Tom literally carried a piece of plywood onto the stage that he stomped even more vigorously than before. The "Stompin'" board became his trademark.

Stompin' Tom sometimes auctioned off his Stompin' boards for charity, with one board selling for fifteen thousand dollars in 2011.

On Canada Day, I'll hoist a few brews for Tom and Frank.

I encourage you to virtually join me and toast our country and the people who have, and continue to make it great.

PART FOUR

Chapter 16

Where is Cell Phone Use Appropriate?

There are more and more rules and regulations that are being introduced to restrict where and when cell phones can be used in society.

It's a good idea.

Schools, cities, and provinces are trying to tackle the spread of cell phone use in public.

However, we may need (dare I say it?) the federal government to provide a national policy or law. I'm not a government-control freak. I think they must step in before rules and regulations about cell phone issues become too complicated.

Distracted driving laws have been enacted in all Canadian provinces. Newfoundland and Labrador (2002) were the first province to adopt a distracted driving law, and Alberta (2011) was the last.

In our highly mobile society, it's difficult to remember what is covered by these new laws when you drive across a provincial border.

For example, I didn't know until my sister-in-law told me that in Alberta the law also applies to people driving while eating a hamburger, putting on make-up, sipping a coffee in addition to using your cell phone.

Here in Saskatchewan, the law applies to using your cell phone (text or in conversation) while driving.

Last summer, the city of Honolulu barred pedestrians from viewing handheld (or portable) mobile devices while crossing a street.

Fines range from fifteen to ninety-nine dollars depending on the number of previous infractions.

"Sometimes I wish there were laws we did not have to pass — that perhaps common sense would prevail," Mayor Kirk Caldwell told reporters. "But sometimes we lack common sense."

Officials cited the rising number of accidents in the tourist-heavy city. If you pardon the pun, this is step in the right direction, but how is the Hawaiian city going to enforce the fines?

Imagine a balding, beer-bellied tourist wearing flip flops and just a pair of shorts texting while crossing the street. A police officer then stops him to write a ticket.

The tourist has no identification with him, so he says he is Justin Trudeau and lives at 24 Sussex Drive in Ottawa!

In my research, I discovered that a school in Collingwood, Ontario, banned student cell phones from their classes. Good for them.

Pretty River Academy told students they could leave their phones in a basket provided or their lockers. Messages can be checked at recesses and lunch breaks.

I also found a four-year-old study on the subject by the Pew Research Center a nonpartisan American "fact tank," based in Washington, D.C.

"People's cellphone use has injected itself into public spaces," the preamble to the Pew study said.

"This has blurred the line between private and public as often intimate and occasionally blustering phone conversations have now become a common part of the background noise during bus rides, grocery shopping excursions, picnics, sidewalk strolls, waits in airport terminals and many other public venues."

To see how people are responding to these changes, Pew asked people about their views on general cellphone etiquette in public.

About three-quarters of all adults, including those who do not use cellphones, say that it is "generally OK" to use cellphones in unavoidably public areas, such as when walking down the street, while on public transportation or while waiting in line.

Personally, I am against cell phone use standing in the checkout line at my neighborhood grocery store or pharmacy (no I don't want to know about nana's dinner plans, what she had for breakfast or about their neighbors' social life as I pay for my prescription drugs.)

I agree with most Americans who do not think it is acceptable to use cellphones in restaurants or at family dinners.

Most also oppose cellphone use in meetings, places where others are usually quiet (such as a movie theatre), or at church.

Where do you stand on the use of cell phones in public?

Chapter 17

Car Keys in the Fridge, TV Remote Control in the Microwave

Do any of these scenarios sound familiar?

You walk into a room and can't remember why you are there.

Ten minutes after you arrive home from grocery shopping, you are frantically searching for your car keys.

The following morning, you open the fridge, and the keys are sitting on a carton of eggs.

Wriggling into your favourite spot on the couch with a plate of freshly made comfort food such as chicken wings or nachos with cheese and hot peppers you reach for the remote control to change the channel to your favourite weekly TV program but it's not in "its place."

After several minutes of searching on, in and around the couch, you decide to warm up the comfort food.

Opening the door, you discover the remote control sitting inside the microwave!

Earlier tonight, I had one of those moments.

After doing the supper dishes, I walked upstairs with a hot cup of tea for my wife (who was checking her personal emails) and carried my notebook in my other hand to leave in my adjacent office.

Mindlessly, I then returned to the main floor of our home and as I sat down in my favourite chair to read a few chapters of a book I realized my notebook was still in my hand and not on my desk.

Shaking my head and laughing at myself I recalled a similar incident a few days ago.

Going into our upstairs bathroom three times within half an hour before acknowledging the real reason for the visit was to retrieve some cough drops for my daily walk!

I did a quick search on the Internet worried that something might be wrong with my aging brain.

The website that first popped up when I searched the words "memory loss" was the Mayo Clinic, a nonprofit organization I knew by name.

Sounds like a credible source. Let's see what they had to say about my concerns.

"Many conditions — not only Alzheimer's disease — can cause memory loss in older adults," began the article on the Mayo Clinic website.

"Getting a prompt diagnosis and appropriate care is important."

That was clear advice that made sense to me.

So, I stopped reading to scribble my doctor's name on my notebook sitting next to my computer.

"Some degree of memory problems, as well as a modest decline in other thinking skills, is a common part of aging," an unnamed clinic researcher wrote.

"There's a difference, however, between normal changes in memory and memory loss associated with Alzheimer's disease and related disorders. And some memory problems are the result of treatable conditions."

That was comforting.

I could almost feel my stress level getting lower as I continued to read.

The Mayo Clinic recommended: "Talk to your doctor to get a diagnosis and appropriate care."

Got it.

"Normal age-related memory loss doesn't prevent you from living a full, productive life. For example, you might occasionally forget a person's name but recall it later in the day."

Been there. Done that, I thought to myself.

"You might misplace your glasses sometime."

Yep, done that too.

"These changes in memory are generally manageable and don't disrupt your ability to work, live independently or maintain a social life."

I also learned about the potential causes of reversible memory loss.

Certain medications or combinations of medications can cause forgetfulness or confusion. A head injury, alcohol interacting with medications and deficiency of vitamin b-12 can also cause memory loss.

"Coming to terms with memory loss and the possible onset of dementia can be difficult," said the Mayo Clinic website.

"Getting a prompt diagnosis is important, even if it's challenging. Identifying a reversible cause of memory impairment enables you to get appropriate treatment."

This makes sense.

Now, why is my doctor's name scribbled in my notebook on my desk?

Chapter 18

Is It a Family Heirloom, Precious Memory, or Junk?

My wife and I have lived in the same house for more than thirty years.

We raised six children, who eventually struck out in the world on their own.

We then cleaned out and repurposed each of their rooms after they had either finished university or had settled into a job and a career path.

We did have a few "boomerangs" (kids who moved back home a few times for a variety of reasons, but usually financial.)

I suspect most readers of *The Senior Paper* also have that one room or closest or drawer(s) where they put "stuff" and, to be quite honest, forget what's there or worse, why we've kept it.

Sitting in our youngest son's bedroom that I now call my study because of the wall-to-wall bookshelves, I began to wonder: what's the difference between a family heirloom, a precious memory for me, and junk?

This thought struck me as I glanced at some of "my stuff" sitting on bookshelves including my yearbooks from Lakewood Secondary School (1969-73).

Yes, "back then," high school in Ontario was from Grade 9-13 (most textbooks we used in Grade 13, were also used in many first-year university courses!)

I digress. Sorry.

In the bottom of the middle section of my wall of bookshelves are traces of my entertainment centre growing up in Kenora, Ontario.

Sitting beside the green Viking portable record player purchased from Eaton's by mail order catalogue, are boxes and boxes of vinyl records (33s, 45s, and 78s).

The state-of-the-art record player for 1965 had four speeds and still has several of those yellow plastic discs to insert into 45s so the music or story could be played on a traditional long playing (LP) turntable.

The fourth speed was 16 RPMs (Revolutions Per Minute), but I don't have any of those records remaining. Do you?

I can't play any of my vinyl records that I have because over the years I lost the needle for the record player and haven't bothered to see if it's something that can be inexpensively found and purchased.

Because I was a reporter for most of professional life, I was a "pack rat" and kept many of my tools of my trade: a portable typewriter I used during the 1978 Saskatchewan general election (and a black and white photograph of me typing away on NDP leader Allan Blakeney's campaign bus); a bag with my 35-millimetre (mm) Nikon camera and lenses.

Several three-ring binders containing strips of black and while negatives (which translates into thousands of photographs by the way).

Every "PRESS PASS" I was issued (beginning with CKPG radio and TV in Prince George, B.C., and major sporting events such as the Commonwealth and summer Olympic games) and business cards (ending with my last full-time job as director of communications with an environmental non-government organization in 2013).

Looking around this room, the only items of which I am certain have a home after me are the hundreds of hardcover and paperback books.

One of our sons has agreed to "save these" if I should pass away before my wife and promised to preserve (and hopefully read) most of them.

There is no real sense of urgency for me to make the hard choice between what is a family heirloom, a personal precious memory or junk now.

It's just a meandering question that popped into my head; a thought I suspect many readers have either had to answer because of voluntary (or involuntary downsizing) or will soon face.

I'll probably avoid opening this can of worms by keeping everything I now have but being very prudent in any additions, especially books during the upcoming garage sale season!

What's the difference between a family heirloom, a precious memory for me, and junk?

I don't know and it may be a problem I may never answer.

Chapter 19

'In Flanders Fields'
Honours the Fallen

We are the dead.

I do not recall how old I was the first time I heard or read that sentence from the poem *In Flanders Fields*, but it echoes in my mind every November.

A long, long time ago when I was a high school senior, I was selected to read the poem during the school's Remembrance Day assembly.

Our senior class was a closely knit group and we wanted to make the assembly a memorable event for the Grade 9-13 students.

This was during the Vietnam War.

I was among the male students who had shoulder-length hair. Many of the female students wore mini-skirts or hot pants away from school.

The Remembrance Day assembly was a special effort to show our generation genuinely cared for those who gave their lives.

We began with a colour guard dramatically entering through the back doors of the gymnasium, the sound of their boots echoing as they marched the Canadian and British colours to the front of the gymnasium.

With military precision they stopped, did an about turn and stood at ease.

This group was comprised of fellow high school students who were in the army, air force and navy cadet programs (as well as few "older boys" who were enlisted in the Canadian military reserve with the Royal Canadian Artillery.)

There were a few obligatory speeches from the principal and local politicians, I vaguely recall, then it was my turn.

"In Flanders Fields the poppies blow, between the crosses, row on row," I began reading the 92-word poem.

When I read the opening sentence of the second stanza, a chill ran up my spine and multiplied into goosebumps.

"We are the dead."

I paused, looked up briefly with as sombre a look as a nineteen-year-old could muster and then continued.

"Short days ago, we lived, felt dawn, saw sunset glow."

The rest is a blur in my mind's eye except no one stirred in their steel chairs or on the wooden bleachers when I was finished.

The last time I wrote about Remembrance Day in this newspaper was almost a decade ago so I thought it would be alright to touch on the subject again this month.

"The tradition of wearing poppies in honor of Canada's war dead originates from the poem *In Flanders Fields*, written in 1915 by Lieutenant-Colonel John McCrae, who was born in Guelph, Ontario," I wrote in my November 2013 Senior column.

McCrae, a Canadian Medical Officer during the First World War, was inspired to write the poem after presiding over the funeral of friend and fellow soldier Alexis Helmer, who died in the Second Battle of Ypres in Belgium, my column continued to explain.

Fellow soldiers retrieved the poem after McCrae, unsatisfied with his work, had thrown it away.

In Flanders Fields was first published on December 8 of that year in the London-based magazine *Punch*.

Today, it is often recited at school assemblies (pre-pandemic), public events and on various media platforms.

Originally called Armistice Day, Remembrance Day commemorates the end of the First World War, often called "the War to end all Wars," on Monday, November 11, 1918, at 11:00 A.M. (the eleventh hour of the eleventh day of the eleventh month).

Two minutes of silence continues to be observed in countries such as Australia, Britain, France, and Canada.

Remembrance Day is a statutory holiday in every province and territory except in Manitoba, Ontario, Québec, and Nova Scotia.

There have been twenty "wars" since World War I, said the Britannica website including the Iraq war (2003-11), the Falkland Islands War (1982), Vietnam War (1954-75) and World War II (1939-45).

A *New York Times* article said at least one hundred and eight million people were killed in wars in the twentieth century. About sixty-five thousand of those people were Canadians who died in World War I.

Remembrance Day is not about celebrating war.

It's a sombre reminder of those fallen -- *We are the dead.*

Chapter 20

Learned to Poach Eggs for a Cub Scout Badge

My love of poached eggs can be traced to a Saturday morning in the mid 1960s when I was about ten years old.

Making a poached egg was one of the tasks I was required to complete to earn my House Orderly Badge as a member of the 10th Cub Pack in Kenora, Ontario.

So, under the watchful eyes of my mother and grandmother I cracked an egg on the edge of our cast iron frying pan.

However, because I struck it too hard, most of the egg splattered onto the top of our wood burning stove before I could gently open the shell to place the egg into the boiling water inside the frying pan.

My face flushed with embarrassment. They consoled me.

"Try again, Joey," they chimed in unison, my mother in English and my grandmother in our "house-language" a blend of Polish-Ukrainian-German.

Both the second and third attempts to make poached eggs also were not successful.

After I scraped my disasters from the surface of the stove, I gently cracked the fourth egg and into the boiling water it went.

Minutes later I lifted my first poached egg from the water with a large soup spoon and onto a piece of toast which I also had made on the top of the wood-burning stove.

I was no chef, but I did get the job done.

This incident popped into my mind this morning when I was making my regular breakfast – two poached eggs, toast, black coffee with a side of cottage cheese.

It's a lot easier making poached eggs now because my wife has bought me an "egg poacher pan."

Yes, from time to time I still crack the eggs too hard on the side of the pan.

Today's poached eggs look almost perfect unlike a squashed octopus I produced trying to earn my badge for Cubs years ago.

I also developed leadership skills as a member of the 10th Kenora Pack that met Thursday nights in the basement of the Notre Dame du Portage Roman Catholic Church.

Our groups or lairs were identified by colours: green, blue, white, etc.

I was in the tawny group, rising to the 'rank' of sixer (meaning leader of that group of six boys).

Our Cub Pack season mirrored the school year, so we began in September and wrapped up in June.

When I turned eleven in January, I couldn't join or "move up" to scouts because it was in the middle of their year, so I became "the Senior Sixer" for the 10th Kenora Pack.

Cub activities also mirrored the seasons.

Group hikes were in the autumn and spring. Snowshoeing in the winter. Throughout the year we were encouraged to earn a variety of badges which we proudly sewed onto the sleeves of our jerseys.

Changes in scouting have reflected changes in Canadian society over the past half century.

Boy Scouts of Canada now is called Scouts Canada, has become co-ed and offers more age groups than ever.

Depending on where you grew up and the size of your community you may have had the opportunity to participate in organizations such as Cubs and Scouts, Brownies and Girl Guides or 4-H (head, heart, hands, health) clubs.

Community-based organizations help form the fabric of our society.

Each has their own ritual and rules.

I vaguely recall The Grand Howl at the end of our Thursday night meetings.

Details drift through the windmills of my mind like a leaf floating on an autumn breeze.

"DYB, DYB, DYB, DYB" one Cub would shout the abbreviation in Cub "language" for Do Your Best.

The entire pack would respond: "We'll DOB, DOB, DOB, DOB," meaning "We'll Do Our Best (DOB)."

Each month in the pages of *The Senior Paper* I have done my best to share my experiences with you, even where my love of poached eggs began!

PART FIVE

Chapter 21

Fifteen Dozen Perogies Auctioned for $1,250!

Osage (pop. 20) is about an hour's drive southeast of Regina but is a community that is at the heart of the fabric of rural Canada.

One recent Saturday night, my wife Carla and I took the drive to support a *Funds for Friends* event for her cousin Ed who was about to begin his battle with cancer that began in his colon and had spread to his liver.

We thought we were going to just another medical fund-raiser. Instead, we were able to experience the heart and soul of what is good and just about rural Canada.

In short, where I come from, people matter more.

A light rain helped boost attendance to more than three hundred. Farmers couldn't work their fields.

Instead, they came with mud on their tires and hope in their hearts to lend a helping hand.

They came too with their chequebooks open, and broad, often toothless grins beneath their favourite farm implement dealer's baseball cap or Stetson.

We huddled in the same community hall which once was a Quonset to share stories and bid on live and silent auction items.

Anyone who has attended a live auction at a fundraiser can recall one item that generates an unusually large amount of money compared with its intrinsic value.

When I was president of the Saskatchewan Nurses' Foundation, a bidding war always erupted at the registered nurses' annual convention over the ugliest pair of socks I had ever laid eyes on.

Yet, it was the stuff from which legends grew.

The Legend of Osage belongs to my brother-in-law, Denis Sidloski, who farms southwest of Weyburn. He is a generous, caring, church-going individual who often begins a response to a question this way: "Well, the way I figure it is …"

If you're lucky, his narrative may last only ten minutes!

On this particular Saturday night, he didn't do any talking. He just smiled through his furry grayish beard at Shelby, the girlfriend of his youngest son, Quinn, a pilot in training, and nodded his head when the live auction featured their coveted prize.

Evelyn, the mother-in-law of Ed who had started his cancer journey, had donated two batches of fifteen dozen perogies. Shelby wasn't certain she could get the batch in the silent auction and Denis stepped up with his toothy smile and wallet in the live auction.

Before long, Ray, the auctioneer, and another cousin-in-law of mine, had the price up to five hundred dollars which pushed a gaggle of would-be bidders to the sideline. It was a dual between Denis and Paul, a man with a fire hydrant build, sporting a black t-shirt boasting about the volunteer work he had done with the troupe of belly dancers that had performed twice that night.

Up and up the bidding went faster than a male mallard startled as you kicked up the dust speeding past his marshland home en route to yours.

Finally, the bidding stopped. Denis was the "winner" at one thousand two hundred and fifty dollars. Everyone in the hall applauded and cheered.

Less than an hour later, Denis donated the perogies back to organizers.

They interrupted the music from the live band and within a minute of furious bidding the fifteen dozen perogies brought another one thousand one hundred and ten dollars for the cause.

As for Shelby, she sat shivering inside the tent waiting for the silent auction bidding to end. She wanted the second batch of perogies. Every time someone bumped up her bid by five dollars (the minimum), she'd wait until they had gone back inside the hall, and she'd quickly scratch out another bid.

Her winning bid was one hundred and sixty-five dollars. Everyone was a winner on this Saturday night.

Where I come from, people matter more.

It's called Canada.

Chapter 22

Witnessed Dramatic 1973 Bank Robbery in Kenora, Ont.

Time cannot erase some of the most poignant memories we have etched in the recesses of our brain regardless of how many years have passed since the event.

I can remember the look of joy and elation on my wife's face in the delivery room when I told her she had just given birth to a baby girl, our third child. Jenna will be 23 next month.

I can remember the series of events taking Carla to the hospital for the birth of our first son, Ahren, who will be 28 in October.

It was thirty-five years ago this month that I witnessed one of the most dramatic bank robberies in Canadian history. I was nineteen and walking home from Lakewood Secondary School in my hometown of Kenora, Ont.

My friends and I rounded the corner by the red brick post office, built in 1895, to see Main Street blocked off by police cars and hundreds of people standing around.

We thought we were walking into a scene from a Hollywood movie. Gun-toting police from three authorities were running around.

There was virtually no crowd control. There was no communication with the crowd.

We learned from people who were already standing around that a bank robbery was in progress.

"In our town?"

We couldn't believe it.

There were four banks within a block of each other on Main Street. The robber had selected the Canadian Imperial Bank of Commerce, located about a third of the block down Main Street in the downtown.

We stood on the steps of Pitt's Clothing Store at the corner of First Avenue and Main Street.

As teenagers, we laughed and joked about the situation. There were hundreds and hundreds of people watching.

We'd grown up in the logging and tourist town with nothing more eventful happening than our entire senior class skipping school to watch the final game of the 1972 Canada-Russia hockey series the previous fall.

Then, a green Chevrolet half-ton truck rounded the corner of Second Avenue and Main, the police moved their vehicles back, the crowd parted, and it eased up to the entrance of the bank, double parking with the driver sliding out.

"Oh, oh," I uttered without thinking.

"What's wrong?" asked my friend, Maureen Olson, now a high school teacher in Winnipeg.

"That's not a just another town employee. That's Constable Don Milliard going into the bank," I replied.

I caught some movement to my right.

Sergeant Bob Letain of the Kenora Police Service was pulling his hunting rifle, a .308 bolt-action, Winchester, from a leather carrying case, starting to kneel behind the police cruiser about ten metres from us.

"Be ready to hit the ground," I said to my friends. "If something happens, don't run, because the chance of getting hit by bullets or flying debris is greater if you're standing up."

"You're nuts, Joe," they said. "Nothing is going to happen. This is a small town in northern Ontario. Nothing happens here."

I thought back to my training as a member of the Royal Canadian Artillery reserves and positioned myself behind my friends.

Just then the robber, wearing a black balaclava emerged from the bank with Constable Millard carrying a dark green duffle bag.

As the robber went to open the door on the passenger side, you could see he had something strapped to his chest beneath his coat and a clothespin in his mouth.

Sergeant Letain fired through the open windows of the police car. The crack of his rifle sent everyone scrambling and I tackled my friends so they wouldn't get hit.

Then, the retort echoed, and the bomber let the "dead man's switch" go in his mouth, igniting the six sticks of dynamite.

Flesh, blood, money, and glass flew everywhere.

I remember where I was thirty-five years ago this month and it is the subject of my next book, *The Devil's Gap.*

Chapter 23

Today is a Great Day – I Woke Up!

Before I get into the meat of this column, I must declare a conflict of interest.

Over the years, I have battled cancer twice through a combination of thirteen operations, thirty radiation treatments (each time I was "zapped" on eighteen locations on my face and jaw) and twelve hours of chemotherapy.

When asked: How Are You? My response since 2006 has been: Today is a great day – I woke up!

I never asked for the odds or probability of "beating" cancer when my journey began ten years ago. I simply sought medical advice on what to do and then did it.

As many of you know, I'm also a deeply religious person. So, I prayed a lot which helped create and maintain a positive mental attitude.

April is the Canadian Cancer Society's Daffodil Month.

I'm urging you to buy a Daffodil pin or a bouquet of daffodils to support Canadians living with cancer.

Did you know that about every three minutes another Canadian is diagnosed with cancer?

Cancer is not a single disease. In fact, cancer is a family of more than one hundred different diseases.

These different kinds of cancer are usually named according to the part of the body (e.g. breast, lung, prostrate) where they first develop.

Cancer develops when certain cells in your body begin to grow out of control. These abnormal cells sometimes form a mass or lump called a tumor. But not all tumors are cancer.

The exact cause of most cancers is unknown. Cancer has many different causes. It may be caused by exposure to tobacco smoke or other poisons, ultraviolet rays from sunlight and the things we eat.

In my case, the doctors never found the primary source of cancer. In both 2006 and 2008 the growth were secondary.

Doing a pre-surgery questionnaire with one of the doctors as I began my second battle this is how I responded when asked I how was feeling: "I'm a physically fit, fifty-four-year-old man who just happens to have cancer."

Cancer can affect people who look after themselves and otherwise are very healthy. It's estimated about one hundred and ninety-six thousand nine hundred new cases of cancer and seventy- eight thousand deaths from cancer will occur in Canada each year.

Let me try to put that number into perspective.

In Saskatchewan, the seventy-eight thousand would be like losing the entire populations of Estevan, Moose Jaw, and Prince Albert to cancer.

In Ontario, it's roughly equivalent to the City of Peterborough or Niagara Falls.

Cancer is the leading cause of death in Canada and is responsible for thirty per cent of all deaths.

Prevalence is the total number of people living with a diagnosis of cancer at a certain point in time.

In 2009, about eight hundred and ten thousand and forty-five Canadians diagnosed with cancer in the previous ten years were alive.

This represents about two point four percent of the Canadian population or one out of every forty-one Canadians.

I was one of them.

The number of newly diagnosed cancer cases in Canada is increasing, but survival rates are also increasing. These improved survival rates account for the growing number of Canadian cancer survivors.

Survival rates vary depending on the type of cancer.

For example, the five-year relative survival rate for lung cancer is seventeen per cent while breast cancer is eighty-eight per cent and prostate cancer is ninety-six per cent.

Between 1992–1994 and 2006–2008, survival rates increased from fifty-six percent to sixty-three percent for all cancers combined.

I know I've shared a lot of facts and figures with you in this column.

To be brutally honest, I've probably provided too many numbers to digest in one session.

Let me urge you, once again, to buy daffodils or daffodil pins this month. I will.

Today is a great day. I woke up!

Chapter 24

Effects of My Open-Heart Surgery Still Felt a Decade Later

It's been ten years since I had open heart surgery, and I still cry.

I don't cry from the pain of the surgery but because of the emotional side effects.

While watching *For the Love of the Game* last night, I suddenly had pouty lips and soon became a blubbering idiot.

Tears began rolling down my cheeks during poignant moments in the 1999 movie staring Kevin Costner and Kelly Preston.

I've seen this movie at least half a dozen times because I love the story line: it follows the perfect game performance of an aging star baseball player.

Baseball is the stage for the movie but it's really a metaphor for life, thus my emotional attachment.

"Forty-year-old Billy Chapel has walked to the mound over four thousand times but tonight he's pitching against time," long-time Los Angeles Dodger baseball broadcaster Vin Scully says as the announcer in the movie.

Pitching against time – aren't we all doing that, trying to squeeze a few more innings out of life, I thought and then the rush of tears swept over me.

Other men and women I know also report emotional side effects after their open-heart surgery.

Peter Miault, my best friend growing up in Kenora, Ontario, had a quadruple bypass a few years before my surgery and he tries to stay away from watching movies that may make him sad or overly emotional.

It's not just Hollywood movies that affect us, cartoons and well-done television shows touch the heart strings and suddenly the tears begin to flow.

There wasn't a lot of information on the World Wide Web to explain why we cry after this very intrusive surgery.

"Open heart surgery is one of the most invasive and stressful procedures doctors perform," says information on a website called heartsurgeryinfo.com. "Emotional side effects of open-heart surgery are to come after the procedure."

In open-heart surgery, the heart is exposed for major repairs. The breastbone is broken (often cracked with a medical instrument that looks like a large pair of wire clippers!) and a heart-lung machine is used to pump blood in place of the heart.

This obviously places stress on the body.

"Living with and through the physical effect of open-heart surgery can be daunting," the website says.

Yeah, right.

Imagine laying in the recovery room with tubes in your chest for drainage.

Painful, yes, but the most pain I experienced was sneezing sitting in my living room a few days later. Every rib bone hurt!

"People who have had open-heart surgery report mood changes as do people close to them."

Dr. Barbara Murphy, the Principal Research Fellow at the Australian Centre for Heart Health, says 80 per cent of patients who undergo a heart procedure such as bypass surgery experience some form of 'cardiac blues' including anxiety, anger, tearfulness, and frequent nightmares.

An article published by the University of Michigan also shed some light on this matter.

"If you feel upset or emotional in the weeks after your operation don't worry – this is a normal reaction," the Michigan article told us.

"Many patients report these feelings up to three months after the operation: Mood swings that may include depression, fear, anxiety, loneliness, helplessness and crying easily for no apparent reason."

I had my open-heart surgery on Monday, Feb. 1, 2014, and walked into our home without any assistance around suppertime five days later.

At that time, I was experiencing a lot of physical pain and didn't realize it would pass within a few months.

My emotional pain – a byproduct of the surgery – can quickly bubble to the surface today when I watch certain movies or hear certain songs.

I've always been a "sentimental guy" but now I cry uncontrollably over the littlest things.

It's a price I'm willing to pay because, so far, I've managed to squeeze another decade of life out of my body!

Chapter 25

Best Days of Our Lives?

I have lots of precious memories from my media days (as a daily newspaper photographer, reporter, weekly newspaper editor and wire service correspondent.)

I enjoyed the adrenalin rush of covering "live sporting events" (Commonwealth Games, Olympics, amateur and professional hockey, etc.) and "breaking news" such as natural disasters (floods, forest fires and tornados.)

I never considered myself to be a good writer. I was a grinder who knew how to ask questions and had this unusual talent for getting people to talk – providing me with colourful quotations for my stories.

Looking back through the sands of time, I see my Media Days more as Media Daze bouncing from job to job and province to province based on professional friendships and the desire to learn.

My copy eventually became crisp and lean.

In my early days, I often struggled to "just tell the story" (especially on deadline facing a blank piece of paper scrolled into my Underwood typewriter.)

From time to time, I created an interesting lead (opening sentence of a story.)

This was the first sentence of a profile I wrote for *The Canadian Press* news agency about a double gold medal Olympic athlete.

"Carolyn Waldo spends eight hours a day upside down in water."

It catches your attention and shows the dedication she had invested to become the best synchronized swimmer in the world (at the 1988 Olympics in Seoul, Korea.)

The best and simplest lead sentence for a print story I have ever read was this:

"A man walked on the moon today."

It was among many dispatches filed by *The Associated Press* (AP) on July 24, 1969, the day American astronaut Neil Armstrong walked on the moon. The AP was a cooperative news agency for newspapers in the United States.

Memories from my Media Daze were triggered by a line delivered by actor Philip Seymour Hoffman in the movie *Pirate Radio* (which I watched for about the tenth time last night.)

"What if these are the best days of our lives?" he asks rhetorically sitting on the deck of a boat converted into a radio station. Its purpose was to broadcast rock and roll music into England, where no radio station was permitted to play this genre at the time (early 1960s.)

Got me thinking and thinking and thinking.

My best Media Days were in the late 1970s and early 1980s covering the Montreal Olympics, Commonwealth

Games, three federal elections and about a dozen provincial elections.

Nothing spectacular about my work, by then I was a solid reporter who could grind accurate, clean copy out hour after hour after hour.

Unfortunately, there is no real competition in the media today because of social media.

Competition made editors, correspondents, photographers, and reporters work harder to literally "beat the other guy."

(Never in my career, by the way, did I ever see anyone run into the newsroom and yell: "Stop the presses I have a scoop!")

For me, the most amazing piece of writing on deadline (that means you must complete and deliver your story to the editor in time for it to appear in the next day's edition of the newspaper) is the November 1963 column Jimmy Breslin wrote about the funeral of President John Kennedy.

Breslin's brilliant prose originally appeared in *The New York Herald* (another now defunct newspaper) but because of technology you can still read it online.

Newsday and *The New Yorker* often appear at the top of searches when you type in Jimmy Breslin + The Gravedigger, he hinted.

Goosebumps rushed up and down my back as I wrote that last sentence.

Trust me. This column is worth finding and reading. It's a reporter writing at his best.

It's the best days of media.

Although I stumble down my Media Daze memory lane from time to time, I firmly believe the best days of my life are still ahead of me.

ACKNOWLEDGEMENTS

A special thanks to Clay Stacey, who, as publisher of *The Senior Paper* in 2005, urged me to become a columnist.

The surprise invitation came at the end of a meeting in which I was proposing he promote my second book *Building Our Future: A People's Architectural History of Saskatchewan*.

I was there to suggest we split the revenue from newspaper book sales. Instead, Clay made a counter proposal.

"I need someone to write a column immediately because I learned just before you walked into my office that our long-time columnist had passed away. Can you provide columns for the next five editions and then we can decide during our summer break if it's good for both of us to continue?"

I agreed and since then I have written more than 200 columns exclusively for the paper.

I also acknowledge the continued support of his son, Dennis and his wife Joyce, for allowing me to continue writing my column when they took over the paper.

Without the support of the Stacey family, *Remember When* would not have become a reality nor would researching and writing columns for *The Senior Paper* become such a fulfilling part of my life.

I appreciate the frequent contacts with subscribers who phone, write or email me with their thoughts about a column or an article they have read in *The Senior Paper* that brought a smile to their faces.

Together, we are a community of like-minded people. Thanks!

BIBLIOGRAPHY

Part One

- 1. Ralko, Joe. "Remember Singing ...CA-NA-DA... We Are 20 million!" *The Senior Paper*, July 2024, Page 3.
- 2. Ralko, Joe. "Seniors now outnumber children in Canada." *The Senior Paper*, September 2017, Page 3.
- 3. Ralko, Joe. "How old would you be if you didn't know how old you are?" *The Senior Paper,* January 2019, Page 3.
- 4. Ralko, Joe. "Millennials more likely to be scammed than seniors." *The Senior Paper,* December 2017, Page 3.
- 5. Ralko, Joe. "Technology Can be Difficult to Master." *The Senior Paper,* June 2024

Part Two

- 6. Ralko, Joe. "I see leaves of green in the heart of winter." *The Senior Paper*, February 2022, Page 3.
- 7. Ralko, Joe. "Remember the sights, smells, and sounds of summer." *The Senior Paper*, July 2019, Page 3.

· 8. Ralko, Joe. "October can be great, but winter is coming." *The Senior Paper*, October 2023, Page 3.

· 9. Ralko, Joe. "Worst part about winter – fewer hours of daylight." *The Senior Paper*, December 2019, Page 3.

· 10. Ralko, Joe. "Christmas shopping has changed dramatically in our lifetime." *The Senior Paper,* December 2021, Page 3.

Part Three

· 11. Ralko, Joe. "So, You Think You Know Canada's History?" *The Senior Paper*, July 2015, Page 3

· 12. Ralko, Joe. "Happy Sixteenth Birthday to Me!" *The Senior Paper,* January 2020, Page 3.

· 13. Ralko, Joe. "Inventions and other stuff you ought to know about Canada." *The Senior Paper,* July 2020, Page 3.

· 14. Ralko, Joe. "How to speak Canadian from Eh to Zed." *The Senior Paper,* July 2023, Page 3.

· 15. Ralko, Joe. "Toast Your Favourite Canadian This Summer." *The Senior Paper*, July 2013, Page 3

Part Four

· 16. Ralko, Joe. "Where is cell phone use appropriate?" *The Senior Paper*, April 2018, Page 3.

· 17. Ralko, Joe. "Car keys in the fridge, TV remote in the microwave." *The Senior Paper,* May 2018, Page 3.

- **18.** Ralko, Joe. "Is it a family heirloom, precious memory, or junk?" *The Senior Paper,* March 2020, Page 3.
- **19.** Ralko, Joe. *"In Flanders Fields* honours the fallen." *The Senior Paper,* November 2021, Page 3.
- **20.** Ralko, Joe. "Learned to poach eggs for a cub scout badge." *The Senior Paper,* September 2024, Page 3.

Part Five

- **21.** Ralko, Joe. "Fifteen dozen perogies auctioned off for $1,250!" *The Senior Paper,* September 2012, Page 3.
- **22.** Ralko, Joe. "I witnessed dramatic Kenora bank robbery in 1973." *The Senior Paper*, May 2008, Page 3.
- **23.** Ralko, Joe. "Today is a great day – I woke up!" *The Senior Paper,* April 2016, Page 3.
- **24.** Ralko, Joe. "Effects of open heart surgery still felt a decade later." *The Senior Paper*, February 2024, Page 3.
- **25.** Ralko, Joe. "Are These the Best Days of Our Lives?" *The Senior Paper,* November 2022, Page. 3.

About Joe Ralko

Joe Ralko has written more than 200 columns exclusively for *The Senior Paper* since 2005.

He has earned his living as a writer for more than four decades, first as the sports editor of the daily newspaper in his hometown of Kenora, Ontario and then as an editor, reporter and photograph for a variety of other media outlets in three provinces before joining *The Canadian Press* news agency where he earned a pair of nominations for National Newspaper Awards (NNAs) as a correspondent.

This is his fifth nonfiction book.

He welcomes your ideas and thoughts via email jralko@myaccess.ca

<u>Also By Joe Ralko:</u>
Regina: Ready for the New Millennium (2000)
Building Our Future: A People's Architectural History of Saskatchewan (2005)
The Devil's Gap: The Untold Story of Canada's First Suicide Bomber (2017)
There's So Much More We Can Be (2021)
<u>Audio only</u>
From Horseback to Professor to Premier and Beyond: the audio memoirs of Grant Devine (2024)

About The Senior Paper

Founded in 1977, *The Senior Paper* is a paid-subscription periodical published the first Monday of each month eleven times per year (every month except August).

Articles in the periodical are submitted by seniors about their own life experiences.

Joe Ralko is the paper's longest contributing columnist.

The Senior Paper is printed in large, easy-to-read type with a clutter-free format. To learn more visit https://www.the-seniorpaper.com/ .

To subscribe or order to a FREE sample copy of the paper visit https://theseniorpaper.com/online/subscription-department/